I0821136

This book is presented to:
From:
Date:

YOUR WORTH NEVER WAVERS

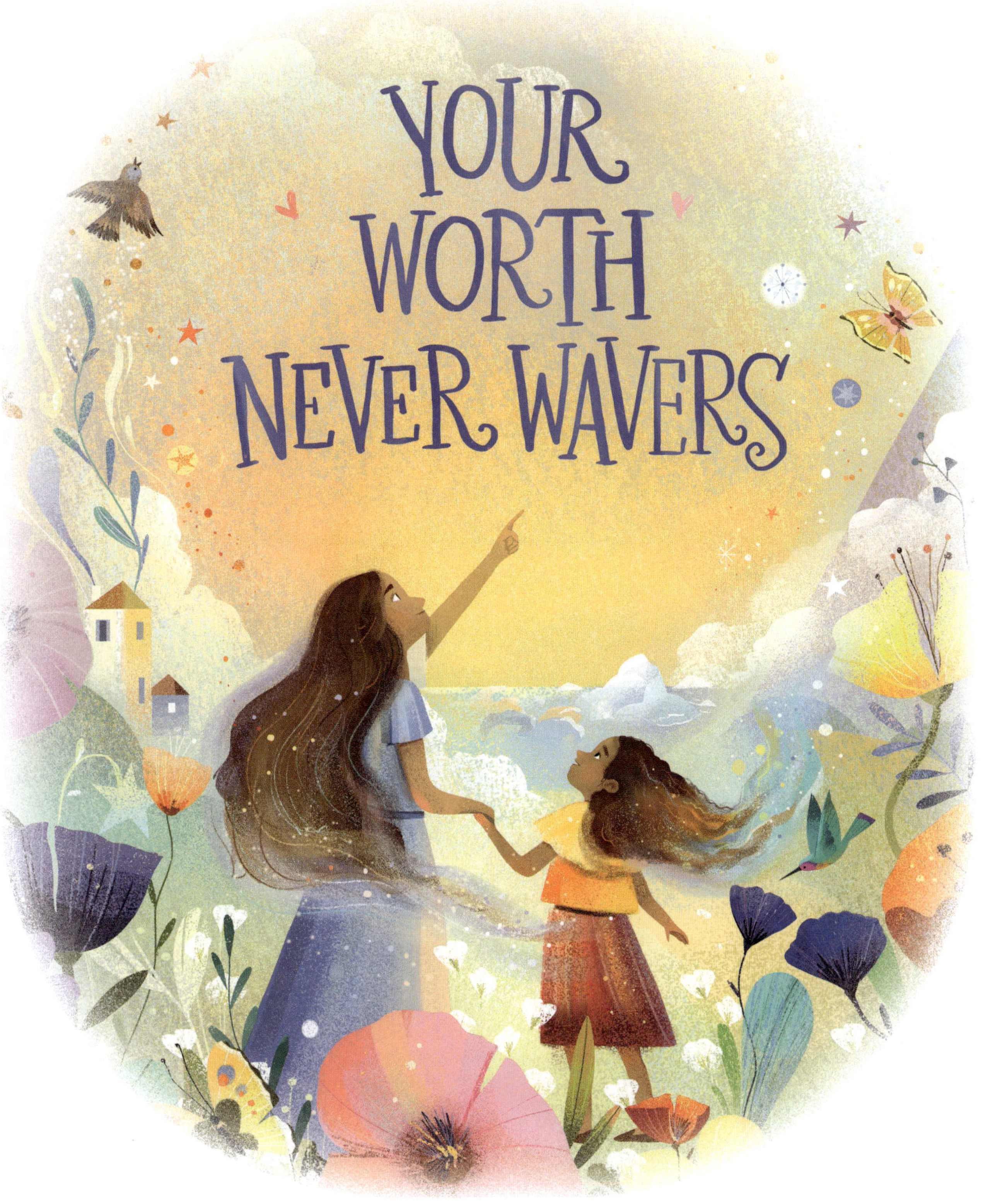

Laura Wifler

B&H kids
Brentwood TN

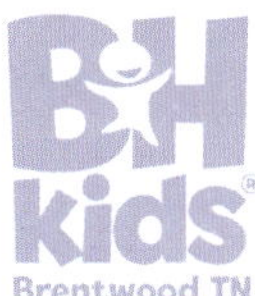

To my own daughters,
Colette and Eden,
and every other girl in the world:
May you never forget that
you are worthy and beautiful,
all the way through.

Published by B&H Publishing Group, Brentwood, Tennessee

Dewey Decimal Classification: C155.2
Subject Heading: SELF-ESTEEM \ GOD \ CREATION
ISBN: 979-8-3845-1561-6
Manufactured by Asia Pacific, Shenzhen, Guangdong, China, in September 2025
2 3 4 5 6 7 • 29 28 27 26 25

Come over beside me,
my sweet, darling girl.
Yes, you, you're the one
full of giggles and twirls.

You're a talent at reading
and doodling art,
And your great superpower
is your kindness of heart.

Do you know, my sweet girl, just how much I love you?
You are worthy and beautiful, all the way through.

Do you know how I know? How I'm sure beyond measure?
Come over, I'll show you. Let's travel together.

Here's a pineapple,
it takes two years to grow strong.

Here's a glacier,
the ice is a hundred miles long.

Here's a tiger,
fierce stripes are stamped onto its skin.

Here's a hummingbird,
flying backward in the wind.

The same God who made
both the otter and pearl,
Is the God who
made you—
yes you, my
sweet girl.

You're made in His image;
He knit you together.
Your worth never wavers—
not now, and not ever.

When you wonder your value or question your worth,
Know you're beloved by the God who formed Earth.

Every tree, every bird, every river and fern,
It all watches and trembles—awaits His return.

Here's a snowflake,
each frozen crystal unique.

Here's a mountain,
clouds live at the
tip of its peak.

Here's a star,
a vast island in deep outer space.

Here's a bullfrog,
it leaps seven feet from one place.

Now, there may come a day
when you're not sure what's true—

When your mind starts to doubt
and your thinking gets skewed.

You may feel in your heart a strong tug and a pull.
You may ask, "Am I worthy? Am I beautiful?"

If you wonder or worry
or feel split in two,
Don't fret, my dear child,
here's what you can do.

Turn your face to the wind.
Feel the breeze in your hair.
God's strong love surrounds you;
He's always right there.

Each sunset, each raindrop
is proof of His care—
Though you cannot see Him,
God's in all that's fair.

God's power is matchless—His wisdom, supreme.
Jesus calls you worthy; it's you He's redeemed.

Look to Him when life's hazy, and all will be clear.
Remember His promise: He'll wipe every tear.

So set your eyes on the sky to marvel and wonder,
And feel small as you watch giant clouds roll with thunder.

Feel awe once again for your God and your King,
For His Truth can be seen in each living thing.

Do you know, my sweet girl, just how much God loves you?
You are worthy and beautiful, all the way through.

Do you know how I know? How I'm sure beyond measure?
Come over, I'll show you. Let's travel together.

Here's a redwood,
it stands with the
earth's tallest trees.

Here's a hive,
a sweet home to
sixty thousand bees.

Here's a butterfly,
it transforms in a cocoon.

Here's the ocean,
it rises and falls with the moon.

Feel the warmth of the sun; let your skin know its light.
May it remind you of things true, good, and right.

You're made in God's image; He knit you together.
Your worth never wavers—not now, and not ever.

You are worthy and beautiful
all the way through.
Keep your eyes on our God
who made all of you.

This you can know, and
be sure beyond measure.
Lift your eyes up to Him;
you are His treasure.

Laura Wifler has authored multiple bestselling, award-winning books for children, including *Any Time, Any Place, Any Prayer*, and *Like Me*, and she is the co-author of the bestselling *Risen Motherhood* book. Laura is also the founder of *The KidLit Lab*, where she guides writers in crafting captivating children's books and navigating the publishing process. She lives in central Iowa with her husband and three children. You can find her on Instagram @laurawifler, or at laurawifler.com.